Tony Gonzalez

by Michael Sandler

Consultant: Norries Wilson
Head Football Coach
Columbia University

BEARPORT PUBLISHING

New York, New York

Credits

Cover and Title Page, © AP Images/Kevin Terrell, Shadow Buddies Foundation, and Joseph Sohm/Visions of America, LLC/Alamy; 4, © AP Images/Paul Spinelli; 5, © Wesley Hitt/Getty Images; 6, © Ann Johansson/Corbis; 7, © Fernando Medina/NBAE via Getty Images; 8, © Copyright 2008. Carolyn Wingfield Price Reed; 9, © Mark E. Gibson/Corbis; 10, © Otto Greule/Allsport/Getty images; 11, © David Taylor/Allsport/Getty images; 12, © Hank Young/Young Company; 13, © AP Images/NFL Photos; 14, © Tim Umphrey/Getty Images; 15, © David E. Klutho/Sports Illustrated/Getty Images; 16, © Hank Young/Young Company; 17, © Hank Young/Young Company; 18, © Keith Philpott/Time Life Pictures/Getty Images; 19, © Shadow Buddies Foundation; 20, © AP Images/John Amis; 21, © Kevin C. Cox/Getty Images; 22L, © MCT/Newscom; 22R, © Kevin C. Cox/Getty Images.

Publisher: Kenn Goin
Senior Editor: Lisa Wiseman
Creative Director: Spencer Brinker
Photo Researcher: Omni-Photo Communications, Inc.
Design: Dawn Beard Creative

Library of Congress Cataloging-in-Publication Data

Sandler, Michael, 1965–
  Tony Gonzalez / by Michael Sandler.
      p. cm. — (Football heroes making a difference)
  Includes bibliographical references and index.
  ISBN-13: 978-1-936087-61-7 (library binding : alk. paper)
  ISBN-10: 1-936087-61-8 (library binding : alk. paper)
  1. Gonzalez, Tony, 1976–Juvenile literature. 2. Football players—United States—Biography—Juvenile literature. I. Title.
  GV939.G655S26 2010
  796.332092—dc22
  [B]
                                        2009029852

For more information, write to Bearport Publishing Company, Inc., 101 Fifth Avenue, Suite 6R, New York, New York 10003. Printed in the United States of America in North Mankato, Minnesota.

112009
090309CGB

10 9 8 7 6 5 4 3 2 1

CONTENTS

Sweet 63

The ball was **snapped**. The Kansas City Chiefs' quarterback, Damon Huard, dropped back to pass. He looked into the **end zone** and saw **tight end** Tony Gonzalez racing into the corner. Tony slid behind the Cincinnati Bengals' **defenders**. Damon let the ball fly. Tony reached out and pulled it down. Touchdown!

Now it was time to celebrate! Gonzalez took the ball and slam-dunked it over the cross bar. This was no ordinary score. It was the 63rd touchdown catch of Tony's career, a new NFL record for tight ends.

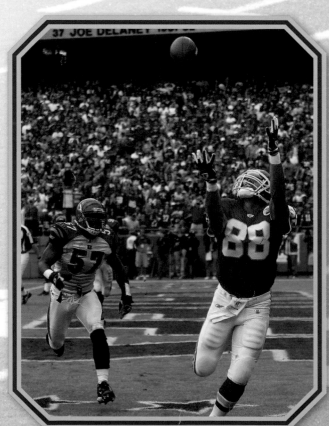

Tony (#88) about to catch the ball and set the NFL record for touchdowns by tight ends

4

Tony dunks the
ball in celebration.

Tony scored his record-breaking touchdown
on October 14, 2007, in the Chiefs' 27-20 win
against the Cincinnati Bengals. Within a year,
Tony set two more career records for tight
ends—most catches and most **receiving yards**.

Building Self-Esteem

Surprisingly, the great NFL tight end didn't start out as a natural at football. "I was awful as a child," Tony said. He remembers being one of the very worst players on his **Pop Warner** team.

It wasn't just a matter of skill. Tony was shy and he wasn't very aggressive. He was also afraid of some of the other kids. Up until middle school, he spent lots of time hiding from bullies.

What changed things around for Tony? Confidence! During the summer after eighth grade, he joined a basketball league and discovered that he was good at the sport. Basketball helped his **self-esteem** grow.

Tony grew up in Huntington Beach, California.

In Tony's very first basketball game, he scored 18 points.

Even as an adult, Tony still enjoys playing basketball.

Two-Sport Player

For Tony, doing well at basketball changed him as a person. "After basketball, well, I got it," Tony said. "I figured it out. I could play football, too." He returned to the sport with a whole new attitude. He was no longer a shy kid. He was now a strong, confident young man.

Tony played both basketball and football in high school. By junior year, he was a key player on the Huntington Beach High School football team. He played both **offense** and defense. As middle **linebacker**, he made tackle after tackle. As a tight end, he caught passes and made blocks.

Colleges across the country began to **recruit** Tony. He decided to go to the University of California at Berkeley.

This is the high school that Tony attended.

During Tony's senior year of high school, in 1993–1994, he was an **All-American** as both a tight end and a linebacker.

The University of California at Berkeley, where Tony attended college.

College Success

At the University of California, Tony continued playing both sports. He was a strong basketball player, becoming a key **sixth man** for the Golden Bears. He even helped the team reach the **Sweet Sixteen** in the 1997 **NCAA tournament**.

In football, he became something more—a superstar. By junior year, Tony was an All-American tight end. When the season ended, he announced his decision to enter the NFL **draft**. Tony was ready to try his skills in the pros.

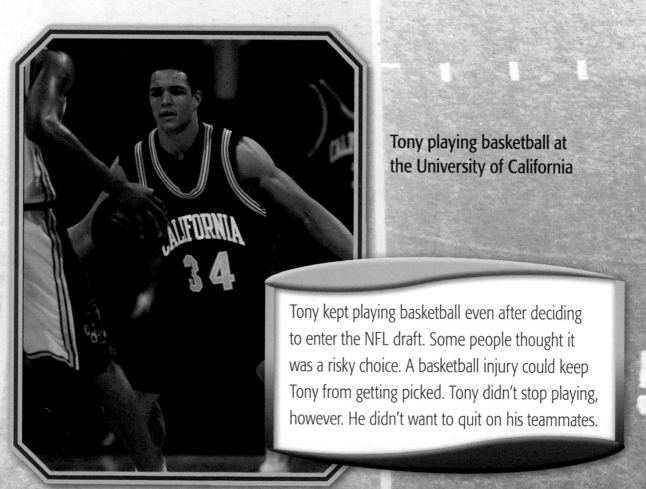

Tony playing basketball at the University of California

Tony kept playing basketball even after deciding to enter the NFL draft. Some people thought it was a risky choice. A basketball injury could keep Tony from getting picked. Tony didn't stop playing, however. He didn't want to quit on his teammates.

In his junior year, Tony caught 44 passes for 699 yards (639 m), more than any other tight end in the country.

Going to Kansas City

The Kansas City Chiefs chose Tony with the 13th pick in the 1997 NFL draft. Tony couldn't wait to start playing. "My first goal is to get to camp and see how good I can become," he said.

After a slow start, Tony became very good. He really began to shine during the end of his second season. In the last five games of 1998, Tony caught 24 passes.

Then, in Tony's third season, he reached a whole new level of play. He caught 76 passes, 11 of them for touchdowns, and was voted to play in the **Pro Bowl** for the first time.

Tony (#88) playing for the Chiefs in 1999

Tony (#87) at the Pro Bowl in February 2000

Tony was the first Kansas City Chiefs tight end ever to make the Pro Bowl.

The Terrific Tight End

Soon, fans, players, and coaches were calling Tony the NFL's best tight end. He excelled at the most important parts of a tight end's job—making blocks and catching passes.

His strength helped him as a blocker. He could knock down defenders and open up the field for running backs and **wide receivers**. His speed and jumping abilities made him an unstoppable pass catcher. Tony twisted and turned high in the air to pull down balls.

Between 1999 and 2009, Tony made the Pro Bowl 10 different times. He also helped the Chiefs advance to three playoff appearances.

Tony (#88) blocks defensive end Adewale Ogunleye (#93) of the Chicago Bears.

Tony leaps to make a catch in a game against the Indianapolis Colts during the 2003–2004 playoffs.

In 2003, Tony led the Chiefs to the **AFC West** championship, the team's first division title in six years.

Helping Others

During Tony's first year as a professional player, he began visiting hospitals. Like many NFL athletes, he spent time with sick kids, trying to cheer them up. During these visits, he discovered that it wasn't just the kids who felt better. He felt happier, too. Ever since, Tony has dedicated his free time to helping others.

To further his commitment, he formed the Tony Gonzalez **Foundation** in 1998. The group's goal is simple—help anyone who is in need, especially children with medical problems or kids who come from poor families. Since the foundation started, Tony has given out Christmas presents to sick children in hospitals as well as football uniforms to kids from families who can't afford them.

Tony visits with a young patient in the hospital.

Tony during a school visit

Tony's foundation works with the Boys & Girls Clubs of America. In 1999, he helped the group in Kansas City get money to build a new football field for kids who live in the area.

Shadow Buddies

It might sound strange—a big, tough NFL player who loves dolls. It's true, however. A special kind of doll called a Shadow Buddy is one of Tony's favorite gifts to hand out. These dolls are given to kids with serious medical conditions. The dolls wear hospital gowns and have been created to look like they have the same diseases or disabilities as the kids they're made for. Some even have stitches as if they've had an operation.

Tony helps support the Shadow Buddies program and gives many dolls directly to the kids himself. The dolls make kids feel like they're not alone with their conditions. A sick child can look at a doll and say, "Hey, it's just like me." Often, the dolls help the kids feel better about themselves and less frightened about their illnesses.

A basket full of Shadow Buddies

Tony poses for a photo after delivering a Shadow Buddy doll to a sick baby in the hospital.

There's even a special Tony Gonzalez #88 Shadow Buddy doll that looks just like Tony. He's the only NFL player to have one.

A New Beginning

Throughout the years, Tony has loved playing football in Kansas City, as well as helping the people who live there. In 2009, however, he decided he needed a change. After 12 seasons with the Chiefs, he asked Kansas City to trade him to a new team. The Chiefs sent him to the Atlanta Falcons.

No one knows if Tony will achieve his ultimate goal with the Falcons—winning a Super Bowl. One thing, however, is certain. Atlanta fans will enjoy watching one of the NFL's greatest tight ends. They will also get to know a person who is very dedicated to two tasks—helping his teammates on the field and helping others off the field.

Tony holds up his new Atlanta Falcons jersey.

Tony (#88) playing
for the Falcons on
September 13, 2009

At the start of the 2009 season,
Tony's 916 catches ranked him fourth
among all active NFL players.

The Tony File

Tony is a football hero on and off the field. Here are some highlights.

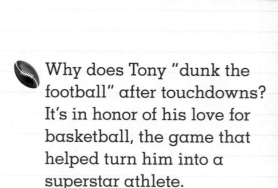

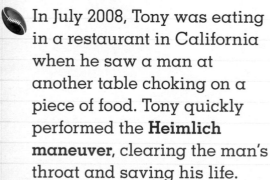 In July 2008, Tony was eating in a restaurant in California when he saw a man at another table choking on a piece of food. Tony quickly performed the **Heimlich maneuver**, clearing the man's throat and saving his life.

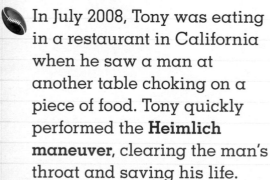 Tony holds the Kansas City Chiefs' record for most games in a row with at least one pass caught.

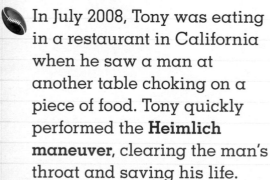 Why does Tony "dunk the football" after touchdowns? It's in honor of his love for basketball, the game that helped turn him into a superstar athlete.

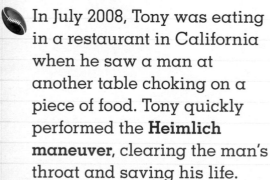 Tony doesn't give dolls to just young people. He also gives out Senior Buddies. These special dolls are made for older people who are in the hospital.

Glossary

AFC West (AY-EFF-SEE WEST) one of four divisions in the NFL's American Football Conference (AFC)

All-American (*awl*-uh-MER-uh-kuhn) a high school or college athlete who is named one of the best at his position in the entire country

defenders (di-FEND-urz) players who stop the other team from scoring

draft (DRAFT) an event in which professional teams take turns choosing college players to play for them

end zone (END ZOHN) the area at either end of the field where touchdowns are scored

foundation (foun-DAY-shuhn) an organization that supports or gives money to worthwhile causes

Heimlich maneuver (HIME-lik muh-NOO-vur) an emergency action performed on a person who is choking by pressing down on the person's upper stomach in order to force out food from his or her windpipe

linebacker (LINE-bak-ur) a defensive player, on the second line of defenders, who makes tackles and defends passes

NCAA tournament (EN-SEE-AY-AY TUR-nuh-muhnt) college basketball's yearly series of games that results in one team becoming the overall champion

offense (AW-fenss) players on a team whose job it is to score

Pop Warner (POP WORN-ur) a group that runs football leagues for kids

Pro Bowl (PROH BOHL) the yearly all-star game for the season's best NFL players

receiving yards (ri-SEE-ving YARDZ) yards gained on a passing play

recruit (ri-KROOT) to persuade an athlete to attend a college and play for its sports teams

self-esteem (*self*-ess-TEEM) pride or respect for oneself

sixth man (SIKSTH MAN) the first basketball player to come off the bench during a game; the best non-starter

snapped (SNAPT) passed back from the center to the quarterback to begin a football play

Sweet Sixteen (SWEET siks-TEEN) the third round of the NCAA tournament

tight end (TITE END) an offensive player who catches passes and makes blocks for other players

wide receivers (WIDE ri-SEE-vurz) players whose job it is to catch passes

Bibliography

Montville, Leigh. "Chief Weapon." *Sports Illustrated* (December 27, 1999).

The Kansas City Star

Sports Illustrated

atlantafalcons.com

Read More

Caffrey, Scott. *The Story of the Kansas City Chiefs.* Mankato, MN: Creative Education (2009).

Gonzalez, Tony, with Greg Brown. *Tony Gonzalez: Catch and Connect.* Kirkland, WA: Positively For Kids (2004).

Hunter, Amy. *Tony Gonzalez (Superstars of Pro Football).* Broomall, PA: Mason Crest (2009).

Learn More Online

To learn more about Tony Gonzalez and the teams he's played for, visit
www.bearportpublishing.com/FootballHeroes

Index